The Arab Dictatorships: The Unfinished Work of the Arab Spring

Copyright Page

TITLE: The Arab Dictatorships: The Unfinished Work of the Arab Spring

1ST Edition

Copyright @ 2023

ISBN: 9798223271154

Table of Contents

The Arab Dictatorships: The Unfinished Work of the Arab Spring

By Roberto Miguel Rodriguez

Chapter 1: The Arab Dictatorships: The Unfinished Work of the Arab Spring

The Arab Spring: A Brief Overview

The Arab Spring, a series of pro-democracy uprisings that swept across the Arab world in the early 2010s, marked a turning point in the region's history. This subchapter provides a brief overview of this transformative period, highlighting its causes, key events, and lasting implications.

The Arab Spring was sparked by a combination of political, social, and economic grievances that had been simmering under the surface for years. Widespread corruption, economic inequality, lack of political freedoms, and human rights abuses were among the factors that fueled popular discontent. High unemployment rates, particularly among the youth, further exacerbated the frustrations of the Arab population.

The catalyst for the Arab Spring was the self-immolation of a Tunisian street vendor named Mohamed Bouazizi in December 2010. His act of desperation and subsequent death ignited a wave of protests in Tunisia, demanding political reform and an end to the authoritarian rule of President Zine El Abidine Ben Ali. The success of the Tunisian revolution inspired similar uprisings in Egypt, Libya, Yemen, Syria, and other Arab countries.

These uprisings, characterized by mass demonstrations, strikes, and civil disobedience, aimed to overthrow long-standing dictators and establish democratic governments. While the initial phase of the Arab Spring saw the swift downfall of leaders such as Ben Ali in Tunisia and Hosni Mubarak in Egypt, the road to democracy proved to be much more complex and turbulent.

In some cases, like Libya and Yemen, the uprisings led to protracted conflicts and power vacuums, with rival factions vying for control. Syria, on the other hand, descended into a brutal civil war that continues to this day, resulting in immense human suffering and displacement.

The Arab Spring also had wider regional and global implications. It exposed the fragility of many Arab dictatorships and shattered the myth of their invincibility. It inspired hope among scholars, politicians, and activists who believed in the possibility of democratic change in the Arab world.

However, it also revealed the complex challenges and obstacles that lay ahead. The rise of extremist groups, the reassertion of authoritarianism, and the destabilization of entire regions were some of the unintended consequences of the Arab Spring.

In conclusion, the Arab Spring was a momentous period in the history of the Arab world, marked by popular uprisings demanding political reform and an end to authoritarian rule. While it brought about significant changes, it also highlighted the complexities and challenges of transitioning from dictatorship to democracy. Understanding the Arab Spring is crucial for scholars, politicians, historians, journalists, educators, teachers, and the public, as it provides valuable insights into the unfinished work of the Arab Spring and the road ahead.

The Impact of the Arab Spring on Arab Dictatorships

The Arab Spring, a wave of uprisings and protests that swept across the Middle East and North Africa region in 2010-2011, had a profound impact on Arab dictatorships. This subchapter explores the repercussions of the Arab Spring on these authoritarian regimes, shedding light on the challenges and opportunities that emerged as a result of this historical movement.

The Arab Spring represented a seismic shift in the political landscape of the Arab world, challenging the longstanding rule of dictators and demanding greater political freedoms, social justice, and economic opportunities. It sparked widespread popular mobilization, with millions of people taking to the streets to voice their grievances and call for change.

In response, Arab dictators employed various tactics to suppress dissent, ranging from violent crackdowns to co-optation and limited reforms. However, the Arab Spring exposed the vulnerabilities of these regimes and shattered the aura of invincibility that had surrounded them for decades.

One of the most significant impacts of the Arab Spring was the empowerment of civil society and opposition movements. Activists and ordinary citizens became more politically engaged, demanding greater accountability, transparency, and respect for human rights. This newfound activism challenged the legitimacy of the dictators and created a space for alternative voices to be heard.

Furthermore, the Arab Spring also highlighted the role of technology and social media in mobilizing and organizing protests. Platforms like Facebook and Twitter allowed activists to communicate, share information, and coordinate actions, bypassing traditional state-controlled media. This posed a significant challenge to dictators' ability to control the narrative and suppress dissent.

The Arab Spring also had far-reaching implications for international relations. It led to a reassessment of Western policies towards Arab dictatorships, with many governments facing criticism for their support of autocratic regimes in the name of stability and counterterrorism. The uprisings also strained regional alliances, as some countries faced pressure to distance themselves from dictators and align with the demands of their populations.

However, the Arab Spring also exposed the fragility of political transitions and the challenges of establishing stable and inclusive democracies. Many countries that witnessed uprisings descended into chaos, with power struggles, sectarian tensions, and violent conflicts emerging in their wake. The subchapter delves into the complexities and lessons learned from these transition processes, highlighting the successes and failures that have shaped post-Arab Spring Arab dictatorships.

Overall, the impact of the Arab Spring on Arab dictatorships cannot be understated. It shattered the illusion of stability and perpetuity that had surrounded these regimes, opening up new possibilities for political change and challenging the status quo. This subchapter provides a comprehensive analysis of the various aspects and implications of the Arab Spring, aiming to contribute to a deeper understanding of the unfinished work of the Arab Spring and its ongoing impact on the region.

The Current State of Arab Dictatorships

In this subchapter, we will delve into the current state of Arab dictatorships, examining the challenges and potential for change that exist within these repressive political systems. This analysis is crucial for scholars, politicians, historians, journalists, educators, teachers, and the public alike, as it provides a comprehensive understanding of the ongoing struggles faced by the Arab world in the aftermath of the Arab Spring.

Since the wave of protests and uprisings that swept across the region in 2011, the Arab dictatorships have undergone various transformations. Some have managed to maintain their grip on power through brutal repression and manipulation of the media, while others have experienced significant upheaval and even toppled regimes. However, the path towards democracy remains unfinished in many countries, as the transition processes have proven to be complex and fraught with challenges.

One of the key factors that continue to shape the current state of Arab dictatorships is the role of women. Despite some progress in women's rights under these regimes, challenges persist, and true gender equality remains elusive. This subchapter will examine the progress made, the obstacles faced, and the potential for change in this critical area.

Economic inequality is another pressing issue within Arab dictatorships. The widening wealth gap has profound implications for social and political stability, as it exacerbates existing grievances and fosters resentment among marginalized groups. By exploring the economic disparities and their consequences, this subchapter will shed light on the underlying factors contributing to the persistence of dictatorships in the region.

Media suppression and censorship are powerful tools employed by Arab dictators to maintain their hold on power. Through control and manipulation of the media, these regimes control the narrative and suppress dissent. This subchapter will analyze the extent of media suppression and its impact on public opinion, political activism, and the prospects for change.

Human rights violations are rampant in Arab dictatorships, with systematic abuses being committed against their own citizens. This subchapter will investigate these violations and their consequences on regional stability, shedding light on the urgent need for international action to address these gross human rights abuses.

Opposition movements and activism have emerged as significant forces within Arab dictatorships, challenging the status quo and demanding change. By studying the various forms of resistance and modes of expression against authoritarian regimes, this subchapter will provide insights into the potential for political change from within.

Furthermore, this subchapter will delve into the dynamics of international relations and alliances with Arab dictatorships, analyzing the complex web of diplomatic interactions and their implications for regional stability.

The role of youth in driving political change within Arab dictatorships will also be assessed, examining the prospects for a brighter future when empowered and politically engaged young people take center stage.

Religious extremism and radical ideologies have also found fertile ground within repressive political systems. This subchapter will explore the contributing factors behind the rise of religious extremism within Arab dictatorships and the implications for regional security.

Lastly, the challenges and successes of countries transitioning from dictatorship to democracy will be investigated. The Arab Spring brought hope for change, but the transition processes have been fraught with difficulties. This subchapter will shed light on the unique challenges faced by countries attempting to navigate the path towards democracy.

In conclusion, this subchapter provides a comprehensive analysis of the current state of Arab dictatorships, addressing various critical aspects such as women's rights, economic inequality, media suppression, human rights violations, opposition movements, international relations, youth engagement, religious extremism, and transition processes. It is an essential resource for scholars, politicians, historians, journalists, educators, teachers, and the public, providing a holistic understanding of the challenges and potential for change within the Arab world.

Chapter 2: The Role of Women in Arab Dictatorships: Examining the progress, challenges, and potential for change in women's rights under Arab dictatorships.

Historical Context of Women's Rights in Arab Dictatorships

The subchapter "Historical Context of Women's Rights in Arab Dictatorships" delves into the progression, challenges, and potential for change in women's rights under the rule of Arab dictatorships. This chapter explores the historical background that has shaped the current status of women's rights in these repressive political systems.

Throughout history, Arab dictatorships have been characterized by patriarchal structures and deep-rooted gender inequalities. Traditional and conservative societal norms have often hindered women's progress and limited their opportunities for education, employment, and political participation. The subjugation of women has been perpetuated by the authoritarian regimes, which have utilized a combination of religious and cultural justifications to maintain their grip on power.

However, it is important to acknowledge that women in Arab dictatorships have been at the forefront of various resistance movements and have played a crucial role in advocating for change. Despite facing significant obstacles, women have persistently demanded equal rights and have challenged the oppressive systems that have marginalized them.

This subchapter delves into key historical events that have shaped women's rights in Arab dictatorships, such as the rise of feminist movements, the impact of colonialism, and the role of religious extremism. It examines the strategies employed by authoritarian regimes to suppress women's activism and the ways in which women have defied these constraints through grassroots organizing, online activism, and international advocacy.

Furthermore, this subchapter explores the progress made in recent years, such as the repeal of certain discriminatory laws and the increased representation of women in political and public spheres. It also highlights the persistent challenges that women continue to face, including gender-based violence, limited access to education and healthcare, and the perpetuation of harmful cultural practices.

By analyzing the historical context of women's rights in Arab dictatorships, this subchapter aims to provide scholars, politicians, historians, journalists, educators, teachers, and the general public with a comprehensive understanding of the complex dynamics surrounding gender equality in these repressive political systems. It sheds light on the potential for change and the role of various actors in advancing women's rights, ultimately contributing to the broader discussion on the unfinished work of the Arab Spring.

Progress and Challenges in Women's Rights

In the wake of the Arab Spring, the role of women in Arab dictatorships has become a subject of intense scrutiny. While some progress has been made in terms of women's rights, significant challenges persist. This subchapter explores the progress made, the challenges faced, and the potential for change in women's rights under Arab dictatorships.

Over the past decade, several Arab dictatorships have taken steps towards gender equality. Saudi Arabia, for example, lifted the ban on women driving and has introduced reforms allowing women to participate in the workforce. In Tunisia, the Personal Status Code was reformed to grant women greater rights in matters of marriage and divorce. These are notable advancements that reflect a changing societal attitude towards women's rights.

However, women in Arab dictatorships continue to face significant challenges. Despite legal reforms, deep-seated patriarchal norms and cultural traditions often limit their ability to fully exercise their rights. Women still face discrimination in education, employment, and political participation. In many cases, they are subjected to gender-based violence and lack access to justice and healthcare.

The potential for change in women's rights under Arab dictatorships is both promising and uncertain. As civil society movements gain momentum and the international community increasingly prioritizes gender equality, there is hope for further progress. Women's rights activists and organizations are working tirelessly to bring about change, challenging societal norms and advocating for policy reforms.

However, the entrenched power structures within Arab dictatorships pose challenges to achieving meaningful change. These regimes often employ repressive tactics to suppress dissent, including targeting women's rights activists. The lack of political will to prioritize women's rights also hinders progress.

To address these challenges, a multi-faceted approach is necessary. Arab dictatorships must enact comprehensive legal reforms that protect and promote women's rights. Education and awareness campaigns should challenge societal norms and promote gender equality. International actors, including scholars, politicians, and journalists, have a critical role to play in amplifying the voices of women's rights activists and advocating for change.

In conclusion, while progress has been made in women's rights under Arab dictatorships, significant challenges remain. Achieving gender equality requires not only legal reforms but also a transformation of societal attitudes and power structures. By acknowledging the progress made, understanding the challenges faced, and working collectively, scholars, politicians, historians, journalists, educators, teachers, and the public can contribute to the ongoing struggle for women's rights in Arab dictatorships.

Potential for Change and Empowerment of Women

The subchapter titled "Potential for Change and Empowerment of Women" delves into the progress, challenges, and potential for change in women's rights under Arab dictatorships. This section of the book sheds light on the critical role women can play in shaping the future of the region and explores the various avenues through which they can be empowered.

In Arab dictatorships, women have historically faced numerous obstacles and systemic discrimination that hindered their advancement. However, the Arab Spring brought about a glimmer of hope for change. The unprecedented uprisings witnessed across the region provided women with a platform to voice their grievances and demand equal rights. While the outcomes of the Arab Spring were mixed, the potential for change and empowerment of women remains significant.

One of the key areas of focus in this subchapter is the progress made in women's rights under Arab dictatorships. It examines the legislative reforms, policies, and initiatives that have been implemented to promote gender equality. It also highlights the notable achievements of women in various fields such as education, employment, and politics. By showcasing these advancements, the subchapter aims to inspire scholars, politicians, historians, journalists, educators, teachers, and the public to recognize the potential for positive change.

However, the subchapter also acknowledges the challenges that persist in the fight for women's rights. It analyzes the deep-rooted cultural and societal norms that perpetuate gender inequality and restrict women's empowerment. It explores the barriers women face in accessing education, healthcare, and economic opportunities. Moreover, it critically examines the role of patriarchal systems in maintaining the status quo and limiting progress.

The subchapter concludes by highlighting the untapped potential of women in driving political and social change. It emphasizes the importance of including women in decision-making processes and leadership positions to create more inclusive and democratic societies. By empowering women, Arab dictatorships can benefit from their unique perspectives, skills, and contributions, leading to more sustainable development and stability.

Overall, this subchapter aims to provide a comprehensive understanding of the progress, challenges, and potential for change in women's rights under Arab dictatorships. It serves as a valuable resource for scholars, politicians, historians, journalists, educators, teachers, and the public interested in addressing gender inequality and promoting women's empowerment in the Arab world.

Chapter 3: Economic Inequality in Arab Dictatorships: Exploring the widening wealth gap and its implications for social and political stability.

The Causes and Consequences of Economic Inequality

In the wake of the Arab Spring, one of the most pressing issues facing the Arab dictatorships is the rampant economic inequality that plagues their societies. This subchapter will delve into the root causes of this inequality and examine its wide-ranging consequences for social and political stability in the region.

At its core, economic inequality in Arab dictatorships can be attributed to a combination of factors. First and foremost, the concentration of power and wealth in the hands of a few ruling elites has created a system of crony capitalism, where economic opportunities are limited to those with political connections. This has led to a significant wealth gap, with a small minority controlling the majority of the region's resources and wealth.

Additionally, the lack of transparent governance and accountability in these dictatorships has perpetuated corruption and hindered economic development. The absence of checks and balances allows rulers to amass vast fortunes at the expense of their citizens, exacerbating the inequality divide.

The consequences of this economic inequality are far-reaching. On a societal level, it breeds resentment and disillusionment among the marginalized majority, leading to social unrest and political instability. The Arab Spring itself can be seen as a direct response to the economic disparities and lack of opportunities faced by the masses.

Moreover, economic inequality has severe implications for political stability. The ruling elites, fearful of losing their privileges, often resort to repressive measures to maintain control. This includes suppressing dissent, censoring the media, and violating human rights. These actions not only perpetuate a cycle of oppression but also fuel radical ideologies and religious extremism, as disenfranchised individuals seek alternative means of expressing their grievances.

Addressing economic inequality in Arab dictatorships is crucial for achieving long-term stability and prosperity in the region. This requires implementing comprehensive reforms that promote inclusivity, transparency, and accountability. Economic policies should focus on creating equal opportunities for all citizens, regardless of their social or political affiliations. Additionally, investing in education and job creation can help alleviate poverty and reduce the wealth gap.

Furthermore, international actors play a significant role in addressing economic inequality. By promoting fair trade practices, providing aid to marginalized communities, and supporting grassroots movements advocating for economic justice, the international community can contribute to creating a more equitable and stable region.

In conclusion, economic inequality in Arab dictatorships is a complex issue with profound implications for social and political stability. By understanding its causes and consequences, scholars, politicians, historians, journalists, educators, teachers, and the public can contribute to the ongoing discussions and efforts aimed at addressing this pressing challenge.

Social and Political Implications of Economic Inequality

The subchapter titled "Social and Political Implications of Economic Inequality" explores the widening wealth gap within Arab dictatorships and its profound implications for social and political stability. This chapter delves into the intricate relationship between economic inequality and various aspects of society, shedding light on the underlying dynamics that perpetuate and exacerbate this issue.

Economic inequality in Arab dictatorships has reached alarming levels, with a small elite accumulating vast wealth while the majority of the population struggles to meet their basic needs. This growing disparity has far-reaching consequences for social cohesion, as it leads to increased social unrest, marginalization, and resentment among the masses. The chapter examines how economic inequality fuels social divisions and widens the gap between the ruling class and the rest of society, creating a breeding ground for discontent and social unrest.

Moreover, the subchapter delves into the political implications of economic inequality, highlighting how it undermines the legitimacy of authoritarian regimes. As the wealth gap widens, the ruling elites become increasingly disconnected from the realities faced by the majority, eroding their legitimacy and intensifying public dissatisfaction. This chapter analyzes the strategies employed by Arab dictatorships to maintain their grip on power in the face of mounting economic inequality, including repression, co-optation, and the exploitation of sectarian and ethnic divisions.

Furthermore, the subchapter explores the impact of economic inequality on political participation and democratic processes. Economic disparities often result in the concentration of political power in the hands of the wealthy, stifling the voices and agency of marginalized groups. This chapter discusses the implications of this power imbalance on political engagement, highlighting the challenges faced by opposition movements and activists in their struggle for political change.

By shedding light on the social and political implications of economic inequality, this subchapter contributes to a deeper understanding of the challenges faced by Arab dictatorships. It serves as a valuable resource for scholars, politicians, historians, journalists, educators, teachers, and the general public interested in comprehending the complex dynamics that shape these societies. Through this analysis, readers gain insights into the urgent need to address economic inequality as a fundamental step towards achieving social justice, political stability, and a more equitable future for the Arab world.

Strategies for Addressing Economic Inequality

Introduction:

Economic inequality has been a persistent issue in Arab dictatorships, exacerbating social and political instability. In this subchapter, we will explore strategies that can be employed to address this pressing problem. By implementing effective measures, policymakers, scholars, and activists can work towards creating a fair and equitable society in Arab dictatorships.

1. Redistributive Policies:

One of the most crucial strategies is to implement redistributive policies that aim to bridge the wealth gap. This can be achieved through progressive taxation, where the wealthy are taxed at higher rates, allowing for a more equitable distribution of resources. Additionally, targeted social welfare programs can provide essential services and support to those most in need.

2. Investment in Education and Skills Development:

To tackle economic inequality, it is imperative to invest in education and skills development initiatives. This will empower individuals to acquire marketable skills, access better job opportunities, and improve their socio-economic status. By prioritizing education, governments can equip their citizens with the tools needed to participate in the modern economy.

3. Job Creation and Economic Diversification:

Creating employment opportunities is vital for reducing economic inequality. Arab dictatorships should focus on diversifying their economies, moving away from overdependence on sectors such as oil and gas. By promoting entrepreneurship and supporting small and medium-sized enterprises, governments can stimulate economic growth and generate jobs.

4. Strengthening Labor Rights and Social Protection:

Ensuring fair labor practices and protecting workers' rights is essential for addressing economic inequality. Governments should enact and enforce laws that safeguard workers' rights, including fair wages, safe working conditions, and the right to unionize. Additionally, robust social protection programs can provide a safety net for vulnerable populations, reducing the impact of economic shocks.

5. Encouraging Inclusive Governance and Transparency:

To combat economic inequality, Arab dictatorships must foster inclusive governance and transparency. This entails promoting citizen participation in decision-making processes, combating corruption, and ensuring accountability of public officials. Transparent and accountable governance mechanisms can help prevent the concentration of wealth and promote inclusive economic policies.

Conclusion:

Addressing economic inequality is a critical task for scholars, politicians, and activists in Arab dictatorships. By implementing redistributive policies, investing in education, creating job opportunities, protecting labor rights, and promoting inclusive governance, we can begin to mitigate the widening wealth gap. Ultimately, these strategies will contribute to social and political stability, fostering a more just and prosperous future for Arab societies.

Chapter 4: Media Suppression and Censorship in Arab Dictatorships: Analyzing the control and manipulation of media as a tool for maintaining power.

The Role of Media in Arab Dictatorships

In the Arab dictatorships, media plays a critical role in shaping public opinion, controlling information flow, and maintaining the power of authoritarian regimes. This subchapter delves into the mechanisms of media suppression and censorship employed by these regimes and analyzes their implications for both domestic and international audiences.

Media in Arab dictatorships is often tightly controlled and manipulated by the ruling elites. Governments exercise strict censorship, monitor content, and limit access to information to ensure that their narrative prevails. Independent journalism, critical reporting, and freedom of expression are stifled, leading to a lack of transparency and accountability within these regimes.

One of the key tools used by Arab dictatorships to control the media is state ownership. Governments often own major media outlets, ensuring that their propaganda and narratives are disseminated to the public. Journalists who do not toe the official line face persecution, imprisonment, or even death, creating an atmosphere of fear and self-censorship.

The impact of media suppression and censorship goes beyond the domestic sphere. Arab dictatorships use their control over media to shape international perceptions and maintain diplomatic alliances. By controlling the narrative, these regimes manipulate global opinions, suppress dissent, and present a façade of stability and legitimacy.

The role of social media in Arab dictatorships is also significant. While digital platforms have provided an avenue for dissent and mobilization, governments have increasingly cracked down on online activism. Internet surveillance, censorship, and targeted cyberattacks have become common tools to silence opposition voices and curtail online freedom of expression.

The consequences of media suppression and censorship in Arab dictatorships are far-reaching. The lack of independent media coverage leads to a distorted understanding of the socio-political realities within these countries. It also hampers the ability of scholars, journalists, and historians to accurately analyze and report on the situation.

However, despite these challenges, brave journalists, activists, and citizen journalists continue to defy censorship and shed light on the truth. Their efforts are crucial in exposing human rights violations, documenting abuses, and challenging the narratives of Arab dictatorships.

Understanding the role of media in Arab dictatorships is essential for scholars, politicians, historians, journalists, educators, teachers, and the public. It enables a critical analysis of the manipulation of information, the suppression of dissent, and the impact on regional stability. By examining media dynamics within these regimes, we can foster informed discussions, advocate for press freedom, and support the aspirations of those striving for a brighter future in the Arab world.

Methods of Media Suppression and Censorship

In the digital age, media plays a crucial role in shaping public opinion and facilitating the free flow of information. However, in Arab dictatorships, the media is often utilized as a tool for maintaining power and suppressing dissent. This subchapter explores the various methods employed by these regimes to control and manipulate the media, highlighting the detrimental consequences for democracy, human rights, and regional stability.

One prevalent method of media suppression is through state ownership and control. Arab dictators establish state-run media outlets that serve as mouthpieces for their propaganda. These outlets disseminate biased information, censor critical voices, and manipulate public perception to ensure the regime's narrative is dominant. Journalists who dare to challenge the official line often face harassment, imprisonment, or even violence.

Another tactic used by Arab dictatorships is the imposition of strict media laws and regulations. These laws are designed to stifle independent journalism and curtail freedom of expression. Journalists and media organizations must obtain licenses, which can be arbitrarily denied or revoked. Content deemed critical of the regime or contrary to its interests is swiftly censored, and those responsible can face severe consequences.

Furthermore, Arab dictators employ digital surveillance and censorship to control online platforms and social media. Internet service providers are coerced into blocking websites, and social media platforms are monitored to identify and punish individuals expressing dissenting views. Online activists and bloggers are subjected to cyberattacks, hacking, and online harassment, further silencing their voices and deterring others from speaking out.

Media suppression and censorship in Arab dictatorships have far-reaching implications. It perpetuates a climate of fear and self-censorship, stifling freedom of expression and hindering the development of a vibrant civil society. It also hampers the ability of citizens to access accurate information, making it difficult for them to make informed decisions and hold their governments accountable.

The international community has a vital role to play in addressing media suppression and censorship in Arab dictatorships. Scholars, politicians, historians, journalists, educators, teachers, and the public must raise awareness about these issues, advocate for press freedom, and support independent media outlets and journalists. By shining a light on the methods employed by these regimes, we can work towards dismantling the systems of control and manipulation, ultimately fostering democratic governance, human rights, and regional stability.

Media Resistance and Strategies for Freedom of Expression

In the midst of Arab dictatorships, the role of media becomes pivotal in challenging the status quo and striving for a more open and democratic society. This subchapter explores the various forms of media resistance and strategies employed by individuals and organizations to assert their freedom of expression despite the oppressive environment.

Media suppression and censorship have long been tools used by Arab dictatorships to control and manipulate public opinion. However, scholars, journalists, and activists have found creative ways to resist these pressures and ensure that the truth reaches the public. From underground newspapers to online platforms, alternative media outlets have emerged as a crucial source of uncensored information in the face of state-controlled media. These outlets often rely on encryption techniques and anonymous sources to protect their contributors and readers from repression.

Technology has played a significant role in facilitating media resistance. Social media platforms have become spaces for individuals to express dissent, share information, and organize protests. Hashtags and viral campaigns have effectively shed light on human rights abuses and mobilized public support both domestically and internationally. However, these digital tools also come with risks, as governments have increased their surveillance and crackdowns on online activism.

To counter media suppression, international organizations, journalists, and educators have partnered to provide training programs and resources for those working in the media sector. These initiatives aim to enhance the skills and knowledge of journalists, enabling them to navigate the challenges of reporting in restrictive environments. By equipping journalists with tools to protect their sources and themselves, these programs contribute to the resilience of the media landscape and the fight for freedom of expression.

In addition to these strategies, media resistance also involves the active engagement of the public. Citizens play a crucial role in challenging the narratives propagated by state-controlled media by seeking out alternative sources and engaging in critical thinking. Educators and teachers have a vital responsibility in promoting media literacy and fostering a culture of questioning and analysis. By empowering individuals with the skills to discern propaganda from truth, media resistance can thrive.

In conclusion, media resistance and strategies for freedom of expression in Arab dictatorships are dynamic and multifaceted. The combination of alternative media outlets, technological advancements, international support, and public engagement serves as a powerful force challenging the oppressive control of information. By continuing to innovate and adapt, scholars, journalists, educators, politicians, and the general public can contribute to the unfinished work of the Arab Spring and strive for a more open and democratic society.

Chapter 5: Human Rights Violations in Arab Dictatorships: Investigating the systematic abuse of human rights and its impact on regional stability.

Overview of Human Rights Violations in Arab Dictatorships

In the wake of the Arab Spring, the world watched as people across the Arab world rose up against their authoritarian governments, demanding freedom, justice, and human rights. Despite initial hopes for a new era of democracy and respect for human rights, many Arab dictatorships continue to perpetrate severe violations against their citizens. This subchapter aims to provide an overview of the widespread and systematic human rights abuses that persist in these repressive regimes.

Arab dictatorships have long been known for their disregard of fundamental human rights, including freedom of expression, assembly, and association. Dissent is brutally suppressed, with anyone who dares to challenge the regime facing arbitrary arrests, torture, and even extrajudicial killings. The subjugation of political opponents, journalists, and activists has become a hallmark of these regimes, as they seek to maintain their grip on power at any cost.

One of the most egregious violations is the denial of basic civil liberties to women in Arab dictatorships. Despite some progress in recent years, women continue to face widespread discrimination and oppression, including limited access to education, employment, and political participation. The subchapter on the role of women in Arab dictatorships will delve deeper into these challenges and explore the potential for change in women's rights.

Economic inequality is another pressing issue in Arab dictatorships, with a widening wealth gap exacerbating social and political instability. The ruling elites accumulate vast fortunes while the majority of the population struggles to make ends meet. This subchapter will examine the implications of economic inequality and its potential to fuel further unrest and discontent.

Media suppression and censorship are used as powerful tools by Arab dictators to control the narrative and silence dissent. Journalists and media outlets are heavily regulated, with state-controlled media serving as propaganda machines for the ruling regimes. The subchapter on media suppression and censorship will analyze the methods employed by these dictatorships to manipulate information and maintain their hold on power.

The systematic abuse of human rights in Arab dictatorships not only has profound consequences for the individuals directly affected but also for regional stability. By investigating the various forms of human rights violations, this subchapter will shed light on the extent of repression and its impact on the broader Arab world.

It is crucial for scholars, politicians, historians, journalists, educators, teachers, and the public to understand the gravity of human rights violations in Arab dictatorships. By raising awareness and engaging in critical discussions, we can contribute to the unfinished work of the Arab Spring and strive for a future where all individuals in the region can enjoy their basic rights and freedoms.

Impacts of Human Rights Violations on Regional Stability

Human rights violations in Arab dictatorships have profound implications for regional stability. The systematic abuse of human rights perpetuated by these authoritarian regimes creates a volatile environment that fuels social unrest, political instability, and even armed conflicts. This subchapter delves into the far-reaching consequences of human rights violations on the stability of the region, shedding light on the intricate relationship between repression and its impact on the Arab world.

By examining the repercussions of human rights abuses in Arab dictatorships, scholars, politicians, historians, journalists, educators, teachers, and the public gain a deeper understanding of the complex dynamics at play. The Arab dictatorships have long been characterized by a disregard for basic human rights, including freedom of expression, assembly, and association. This subchapter highlights the detrimental effects of such violations on both individual lives and the broader society.

Firstly, the abuse of human rights in these dictatorships undermines trust between the state and its citizens. When individuals are subjected to arbitrary arrests, torture, and extrajudicial killings, a climate of fear and mistrust permeates society. This not only stifles dissent but also erodes the social fabric, leading to increased polarization and a heightened potential for violence.

Moreover, human rights violations serve as a catalyst for radicalization and extremism. The denial of fundamental rights and freedoms pushes marginalized individuals and groups towards more extreme ideologies as a means of resistance. This subchapter explores the factors contributing to the rise of religious extremism within repressive political systems, shedding light on the complex interplay between repression and radicalization.

Additionally, the impact of human rights violations transcends national borders, affecting regional stability. The Arab Spring, for instance, was fueled in part by widespread discontent with human rights abuses and the desire for political change. The subchapter investigates the role of opposition movements and activism in challenging authoritarian regimes, highlighting their potential to shape the regional landscape.

Ultimately, addressing human rights violations in Arab dictatorships is crucial for promoting stability and peace in the region. This subchapter provides a comprehensive analysis of the far-reaching consequences of such violations, offering insights for scholars, politicians, historians, journalists, educators, teachers, and the public. By understanding the impact of human rights abuses, stakeholders can work towards developing strategies for change and supporting the transition processes from dictatorship to democracy.

International Efforts to Address Human Rights Violations

In the wake of the Arab Spring uprisings, the world turned its attention to the human rights violations perpetrated by Arab dictatorships. The international community recognized the urgent need to address these violations and promote accountability, justice, and respect for human rights. This subchapter explores the various international efforts that have been made to address human rights violations in Arab dictatorships.

One of the most prominent international bodies involved in addressing human rights violations is the United Nations (UN). The UN Human Rights Council has established mechanisms to investigate and document human rights abuses in Arab dictatorships. These mechanisms include special rapporteurs and commissions of inquiry that have played a crucial role in shedding light on the extent of human rights violations in these countries. The reports produced by these mechanisms serve as important tools for advocacy and raising awareness about the human rights situation in Arab dictatorships.

Non-governmental organizations (NGOs) also play a vital role in addressing human rights violations. Organizations such as Amnesty International and Human Rights Watch have been at the forefront of documenting and advocating for the rights of individuals in Arab dictatorships. Through their reports, campaigns, and advocacy efforts, these organizations bring international attention to human rights abuses and push for accountability and justice.

In addition to these efforts, international sanctions have been imposed on some Arab dictatorships as a means of pressuring them to improve their human rights records. These sanctions can include travel bans, asset freezes, and arms embargoes. While the effectiveness of such measures is debated, they serve as a clear signal that the international community is not willing to turn a blind eye to human rights abuses.

International courts and tribunals have also played a role in addressing human rights violations in Arab dictatorships. The International Criminal Court (ICC) has jurisdiction over crimes against humanity, war crimes, and genocide. In cases where Arab dictators are responsible for such crimes, the ICC has the authority to investigate, prosecute, and hold individuals accountable.

Despite these international efforts, addressing human rights violations in Arab dictatorships remains a complex and challenging task. Many dictators have managed to evade accountability and continue to suppress dissent and violate human rights with impunity. However, the international community's commitment to promoting human rights and holding perpetrators accountable remains steadfast.

In conclusion, international efforts to address human rights violations in Arab dictatorships have been crucial in shedding light on these abuses and advocating for accountability and justice. Through mechanisms established by the UN, the work of NGOs, the imposition of sanctions, and the involvement of international courts, the international community has shown its commitment to promoting human rights in the region. However, much work remains to be done to ensure that the rights of individuals in Arab dictatorships are protected and that perpetrators are held accountable for their actions.

Chapter 6: Opposition Movements and Activism in Arab Dictatorships: Studying the various forms of resistance and modes of expression against authoritarian regimes.

Historical Background of Opposition Movements

The historical background of opposition movements in Arab dictatorships is a crucial aspect to understanding the current state of affairs in the region. The Arab Spring, which began in 2010, marked a turning point in the history of Arab dictatorships, as it sparked widespread protests and demands for political reform across the Middle East and North Africa.

Opposition movements in Arab dictatorships have a long history, dating back to the early 20th century. During the era of European colonization, nationalist movements emerged in response to foreign domination and sought to establish independent Arab states. These movements, such as the Arab Nationalist Movement and the Arab Socialist Ba'ath Party, gained momentum and support from the wider population, but were often suppressed by colonial powers.

In the post-colonial period, opposition movements continued to challenge the autocratic rule of Arab dictators. These movements were often driven by a desire for political, social, and economic reforms, as well as demands for greater civil liberties and human rights. However, the dictators employed various tactics to suppress dissent, including censorship, imprisonment, torture, and even extrajudicial killings.

The rise of Islamist movements in the 20th century also played a significant role in opposition movements in Arab dictatorships. Groups such as the Muslim Brotherhood sought to establish Islamic states and challenge the secular nature of many Arab regimes. These movements gained popularity among segments of the population disillusioned with the corruption and repression of the ruling elites.

The Arab Spring marked a new phase in the history of opposition movements in Arab dictatorships. The mass protests and uprisings that swept across the region were fueled by a combination of political, economic, and social grievances. Ordinary citizens, particularly the youth, mobilized through social media platforms to demand political change, accountability, and an end to autocratic rule.

However, the initial optimism and hopes for democratic transition were quickly dashed in many countries. Several Arab dictatorships responded to the protests with brutal crackdowns, leading to further violence and instability. Others managed to maintain their grip on power through political maneuvering, co-optation of opposition forces, or external support.

Understanding the historical background of opposition movements in Arab dictatorships is crucial for scholars, politicians, historians, journalists, educators, teachers, and the public. It provides insights into the root causes of political unrest, the strategies employed by dictators to maintain power, and the challenges faced by opposition forces. By examining the historical context, we can gain a better understanding of the unfinished work of the Arab Spring and the prospects for democratic change in the region.

Forms of Resistance and Activism

In the wake of the Arab Spring, the Arab dictatorships have faced widespread opposition and demands for change. This subchapter delves into the various forms of resistance and activism that have emerged in these repressive political systems, shedding light on the struggles and aspirations of the people. Scholars, politicians, historians, journalists, educators, teachers, and the general public will find valuable insights into the dynamics of resistance and the potential for transformative change.

One of the most visible forms of resistance has been street protests and demonstrations. These acts of collective defiance have allowed citizens to express their grievances and demand political reform. From Tunisia's Jasmine Revolution to Egypt's Tahrir Square protests, the power of the masses has been a driving force for change. However, such protests often face violent crackdowns by the security forces, leading to a cycle of repression and resistance.

Another important avenue of resistance is online activism and social media. In the age of information, individuals have utilized digital platforms to mobilize, organize, and disseminate information. The internet has provided a space for dissenting voices to be heard and has played a crucial role in exposing human rights abuses and government corruption. However, regimes have also used digital surveillance and censorship to suppress online activism, highlighting the ongoing battle for freedom of expression.

Civil society organizations and human rights groups have played a vital role in documenting and advocating for change. These organizations provide support to victims of state violence, raise awareness about human rights abuses, and work towards legal and institutional reforms. Despite facing immense challenges and restrictions, they continue to be resilient in their pursuit of justice and accountability.

Artistic expression and cultural resistance have also emerged as powerful tools for challenging authoritarian regimes. Writers, musicians, filmmakers, and artists have used their creativity to critique oppressive systems and amplify marginalized voices. Through their work, they have created spaces for dialogue, reflection, and collective healing.

This subchapter also explores other forms of resistance, such as labor strikes, boycotts, and acts of civil disobedience. It sheds light on the risks and sacrifices made by activists, who often face imprisonment, torture, or exile. Additionally, it examines the role of international solidarity and support for opposition movements, highlighting the importance of global networks in amplifying the voices of those fighting for change.

By examining the various forms of resistance and activism, this subchapter provides a comprehensive understanding of the challenges and opportunities faced by individuals and groups striving for a more just and democratic future in the Arab dictatorships. It underscores the persistent desire for change and the determination of those who refuse to remain silent in the face of oppression.

Challenges and Successes of Opposition Movements

In the aftermath of the Arab Spring, opposition movements in Arab dictatorships have emerged as powerful forces for change, challenging the entrenched power structures and demanding greater political freedoms. However, these movements have also faced numerous challenges and obstacles in their quest for democracy and human rights. This subchapter explores the complexities and dynamics of opposition movements in Arab dictatorships, highlighting both their successes and the hurdles they must overcome.

One of the primary challenges faced by opposition movements is the repressive nature of the authoritarian regimes they seek to dismantle. Arab dictators have a long history of suppressing dissent, using tactics such as arbitrary arrests, torture, and extrajudicial killings to silence their opponents. This brutal repression has not only hindered the growth of opposition movements but has also created a climate of fear and intimidation, making it difficult for activists to mobilize and organize effectively.

Another significant challenge is the manipulation and control of media by the ruling regimes. Arab dictators have utilized media suppression and censorship as powerful tools to maintain their grip on power. They have imposed strict regulations on journalists, stifling independent reporting and ensuring that only pro-government narratives are disseminated. As a result, opposition movements often face an uphill battle in getting their message across and countering the regime's propaganda.

Despite these challenges, opposition movements in Arab dictatorships have achieved notable successes. They have demonstrated remarkable resilience and adaptability, finding innovative ways to communicate and mobilize despite the repressive environment. Social media platforms and online activism have played a crucial role in bypassing government controls, allowing activists to connect, share information, and organize protests.

Moreover, opposition movements have successfully used international pressure as a lever for change. The global community, including scholars, politicians, journalists, and educators, has become increasingly aware of the human rights abuses and lack of democratic freedoms in Arab dictatorships. Through their advocacy and reporting, they have shed light on the plight of activists and put pressure on governments to reform.

In conclusion, opposition movements in Arab dictatorships face numerous challenges in their quest for democracy and human rights. However, they have also achieved significant successes in mobilizing and raising awareness, both domestically and internationally. As scholars, politicians, historians, journalists, educators, teachers, and the general public, it is crucial to support and amplify the voices of these movements, ensuring that their struggles are recognized and their demands for freedom and justice are heard. By doing so, we can contribute to the unfinished work of the Arab Spring and help create a more inclusive and democratic future for the region.

Chapter 7: International Relations and Arab Dictatorships: Analyzing the dynamics of diplomatic relations and alliances with Arab dictatorships.

Historical and Current Diplomatic Relations

Diplomatic relations play a crucial role in shaping the international landscape and the Arab dictatorships are no exception. Understanding the historical and current dynamics of these relations is essential in comprehending the complexities of the region and its impact on global politics. This subchapter aims to provide scholars, politicians, historians, journalists, educators, teachers, and the public with a comprehensive analysis of the diplomatic relations involving Arab dictatorships.

Historically, Arab dictatorships have engaged in strategic alliances and partnerships with various countries, both within the region and beyond. These alliances have often been driven by political, economic, and security interests. For instance, during the Cold War era, many Arab dictatorships aligned themselves with either the United States or the Soviet Union, as they sought to secure military aid and economic support. This led to a deep polarization within the region and intensified conflicts.

In the contemporary context, Arab dictatorships continue to forge diplomatic ties based on their national interests. This has resulted in complex webs of alliances and rivalries. For example, some Arab dictatorships maintain close relations with Western powers, such as the United States and European countries, while simultaneously seeking support from regional powers like Saudi Arabia or Iran.

Furthermore, the Arab Spring uprisings of 2011 had a significant impact on diplomatic relations in the region. The wave of protests and demands for political change challenged the existing power structures and forced many countries to reassess their alliances. Some Arab dictatorships faced international pressure and sanctions, while others managed to maintain their relationships through various means, such as financial aid or political concessions.

It is crucial to analyze the dynamics of diplomatic relations with Arab dictatorships as they have far-reaching implications. These relations can influence regional stability, economic development, human rights, and even the prospects for democratic transition. Understanding the motivations and strategies employed by both the Arab dictatorships and their international partners is essential for formulating effective policies and promoting positive change.

In conclusion, the subchapter "Historical and Current Diplomatic Relations" provides an in-depth exploration of the diplomatic ties involving Arab dictatorships. Scholars, politicians, historians, journalists, educators, teachers, and the general public will gain valuable insights into the complexities of these relationships and their impact on various aspects of the Arab dictatorships. By understanding the historical context and analyzing the current dynamics, stakeholders can better navigate the challenges and opportunities presented by diplomatic relations with Arab dictatorships.

International Support for Arab Dictatorships

In the tumultuous aftermath of the Arab Spring, the role of international powers in propping up Arab dictatorships has come under scrutiny. This subchapter delves into the complex web of alliances, interests, and motivations that have allowed these authoritarian regimes to persist, despite widespread calls for democratic reform.

One cannot fully comprehend the endurance of Arab dictatorships without considering the international support they receive. Scholarly research, historical analysis, and journalistic investigations have shed light on the various factors influencing this support, ranging from geopolitical considerations to economic interests.

For scholars, this subchapter provides a comprehensive exploration of the subject, drawing from a rich tapestry of academic literature and expert opinions. By examining case studies and historical precedents, scholars can gain a deeper understanding of the complex dynamics at play in international relations with Arab dictatorships.

Politicians and policymakers must also grapple with the implications of their countries' relationships with these repressive regimes. This subchapter offers a critical examination of the consequences of such alliances, both for regional stability and for the credibility of those who claim to champion democracy and human rights.

Historians will find valuable insights into the historical context of international support for Arab dictatorships. By tracing the evolution of these relationships over time, historians can shed light on patterns of behavior and identify key turning points that have shaped the current landscape.

Journalists play a crucial role in uncovering the often hidden dimensions of international support for Arab dictatorships. This subchapter offers journalists a wealth of information and analysis to inform their investigations, allowing them to expose the complicity of foreign powers in perpetuating authoritarian rule.

Educators and teachers can utilize this subchapter as a valuable resource to educate their students about the complexities of international relations and the ethical dilemmas faced by national governments. By engaging students in nuanced discussions about the role of foreign powers in supporting Arab dictatorships, educators can foster critical thinking and a deeper understanding of global politics.

Ultimately, this subchapter aims to inform the public about the intricate dynamics of international support for Arab dictatorships. By raising awareness and encouraging dialogue, it contributes to a broader understanding of the challenges faced by those fighting for democracy and human rights in the Arab world.

Implications of International Relations on Arab Dictatorships

International relations play a crucial role in shaping the fate of Arab dictatorships, as the actions and decisions of foreign powers have significant implications for the stability and longevity of these authoritarian regimes. This subchapter aims to explore the multifaceted dynamics of international relations with Arab dictatorships and shed light on the consequences of these relationships.

One of the key implications of international relations on Arab dictatorships is the legitimization of oppressive regimes. Through diplomatic engagements, trade agreements, and alliances, foreign powers often provide implicit or explicit support to dictators, bolstering their position and weakening opposition movements. This not only prolongs the suffering of the citizens under these regimes but also undermines the prospects for democratic change.

Furthermore, international relations can also serve as a means of exerting pressure on Arab dictatorships to improve their human rights records. International organizations, such as the United Nations and various human rights groups, often use diplomatic channels to condemn human rights abuses and call for accountability. While these efforts may not always yield immediate results, they contribute to raising awareness and applying pressure on dictators to address the violations.

Another implication of international relations is the impact on regional stability. Arab dictatorships often engage in proxy wars, support militant groups, or pursue aggressive foreign policies to extend their influence and maintain power. These actions can escalate conflicts, fuel regional tensions, and exacerbate existing divisions. As such, the relations between foreign powers and Arab dictatorships can either contribute to regional stability or exacerbate conflicts and insecurity.

Moreover, international relations also shape the economic landscape of Arab dictatorships. Foreign investments, aid packages, and trade agreements can influence economic policies, exacerbating inequality and widening the wealth gap. As a result, the majority of citizens suffer from economic hardship, while a small elite class benefits from these relationships. This economic inequality not only perpetuates social and political instability but also fuels resentment towards foreign powers seen as complicit in supporting these oppressive regimes.

In conclusion, international relations have far-reaching implications on Arab dictatorships. These relationships can either consolidate the power of dictators or exert pressure for democratic reforms and respect for human rights. Additionally, they can either contribute to regional stability or exacerbate conflicts and insecurity. It is crucial for scholars, politicians, historians, journalists, educators, teachers, and the public to understand these implications and work towards promoting democratic change and regional stability in the Arab world.

Chapter 8: Youth and Political Engagement in Arab Dictatorships: Assessing the role of young people in driving political change and their prospects for a brighter future.

Youth Demographics and Political Participation

The subchapter "Youth Demographics and Political Participation" delves into the role of young people in driving political change within Arab dictatorships, as well as their prospects for a brighter future. The Arab Spring, which saw waves of protests and uprisings across the Middle East and North Africa, highlighted the significant role of youth in challenging authoritarian regimes and demanding political reform.

This section explores the demographics of the youth population in Arab dictatorships, emphasizing their numbers, aspirations, and challenges. With a large percentage of the population being young, the chapter examines how their frustrations with limited opportunities, high unemployment rates, and political repression have fueled their engagement in political activism.

The subchapter also analyzes the various forms of youth political participation, including street protests, social media activism, and involvement in opposition movements. It explores how young people are utilizing digital platforms and technology to mobilize and raise awareness about their demands for political change. Additionally, the section investigates the impact of youth-led movements in shaping the political landscape of Arab dictatorships.

Furthermore, the subchapter discusses the obstacles that young people face when engaging in political activism, such as government crackdowns, surveillance, and restrictions on freedom of speech. It examines the strategies employed by authoritarian regimes to control and suppress youth movements, including internet censorship and the use of force.

The section also explores the potential for a brighter future for young people in Arab dictatorships. It examines the prospects for political reform and democratization, as well as the role of education and youth empowerment programs in fostering positive change. The subchapter highlights the importance of investing in the youth population to ensure their political engagement and participation in shaping the future of their countries.

Overall, "Youth Demographics and Political Participation" sheds light on the crucial role of young people in driving political change within Arab dictatorships. It highlights their aspirations, challenges, and prospects for a brighter future, while also discussing the strategies employed by authoritarian regimes to suppress their activism. The subchapter aims to provide scholars, politicians, historians, journalists, educators, teachers, and the public with a comprehensive understanding of the dynamics between youth demographics and political participation in Arab dictatorships.

Challenges and Opportunities for Youth Engagement

In the aftermath of the Arab Spring, the role of young people in driving political change and their prospects for a brighter future have become increasingly important. Arab dictatorships have long suppressed the voices of their youth, limiting their opportunities for engagement and stifling their potential. However, amidst the challenges, there are also significant opportunities for youth involvement in shaping the future of their countries.

One of the key challenges for youth engagement in Arab dictatorships is the lack of political freedom and space for dissent. Authoritarian regimes have historically targeted young activists, imprisoning and intimidating them to maintain their grip on power. This has created a climate of fear, making it difficult for young people to express their opinions and participate in political processes.

Another challenge is the limited access to education and economic opportunities. Many young people in Arab dictatorships face high levels of unemployment and poverty, which not only hampers their personal growth but also limits their ability to contribute to their communities. The lack of access to quality education further exacerbates these challenges, as it denies young people the knowledge and skills necessary for civic engagement and active participation in the political sphere.

Despite these challenges, there are also significant opportunities for youth engagement in Arab dictatorships. The rise of social media and digital platforms has provided young people with alternative avenues for expression and mobilization. Through online activism, young activists have been able to organize and raise awareness about key issues, bypassing traditional media censorship and reaching a wider audience.

Moreover, the energy and passion of young people can be harnessed to drive positive change. Youth-led movements and protests have been at the forefront of demanding political reform and advocating for social justice. Their determination and resilience have challenged the status quo and inspired others to join the fight for a more inclusive and democratic society.

To fully realize the potential of youth engagement, it is crucial for scholars, politicians, historians, journalists, educators, teachers, and the public to support and empower young people. This can be done by providing them with access to education and economic opportunities, creating spaces for their voices to be heard, and protecting their rights to free expression and assembly.

In conclusion, while there are significant challenges to youth engagement in Arab dictatorships, there are also opportunities for positive change. By addressing the barriers that limit their participation and harnessing their energy and creativity, young people can play a pivotal role in shaping the future of their countries and realizing the unfinished work of the Arab Spring.

Strategies for Empowering Youth in Arab Dictatorships

Introduction:

The youth population in Arab dictatorships represents a significant demographic, one that holds immense potential for driving political change and shaping the future of these nations. However, the oppressive nature of these regimes often suppresses their voices and limits their opportunities for engagement. This subchapter explores strategies for empowering youth in Arab dictatorships, focusing on the importance of education, technology, civil society, and international support.

Education as a Catalyst for Change:

Investing in quality education is crucial for empowering youth in Arab dictatorships. By providing access to critical thinking, civic education, and human rights awareness, young people can develop the necessary skills and knowledge to challenge authoritarianism. Governments and international organizations should prioritize education reforms, ensuring equal opportunities for both genders and marginalized communities.

Leveraging Technology for Mobilization:

The digital revolution has opened new avenues for youth to mobilize and express their grievances. Arab dictatorships have increasingly employed surveillance and censorship to stifle dissent, but young activists have found innovative ways to circumvent these barriers. Empowering youth with digital literacy skills and supporting online platforms for dialogue and activism can amplify their voices and facilitate collective action.

Supporting Civil Society Initiatives:

Civil society organizations play a vital role in empowering youth by providing spaces for expression, skill-building, and networking. Governments should create an enabling environment for these organizations to thrive, including legal protections, funding, and partnerships with international actors. Additionally, fostering intergenerational dialogue and mentorship programs can bridge the gap between youth and established leaders.

International Support and Solidarity:

International actors have a responsibility to support youth empowerment initiatives in Arab dictatorships. This can be achieved through funding programs that promote youth-led initiatives, advocating for human rights and political freedoms, and providing platforms for dialogue and exchange. Scholars, politicians, journalists, and educators can play a crucial role in raising awareness and mobilizing support for youth empowerment.

Conclusion:

Empowering youth in Arab dictatorships is essential for fostering political change and building a brighter future for these nations. By investing in education, leveraging technology, supporting civil society initiatives, and providing international support and solidarity, the voices and aspirations of young people can be amplified. Scholars, politicians, historians, journalists, educators, teachers, and the public must recognize and prioritize the importance of youth engagement in driving political transformation and advocate for their empowerment. Only through collective efforts can the unfinished work of the Arab Spring be addressed and a path towards democracy and stability in Arab dictatorships be paved.

Chapter 9: Religious Extremism in Arab Dictatorships: Exploring the factors contributing to the rise of radical ideologies within repressive political systems.

Historical Context of Religious Extremism

Religious extremism has long been a complex and deeply rooted issue within Arab dictatorships. To understand its origins and implications, it is crucial to examine the historical context that has contributed to the rise of radical ideologies within repressive political systems.

The roots of religious extremism in Arab dictatorships can be traced back to the colonial era, when Western powers exerted control over the region. The imposition of foreign rule and the disruption of traditional social and political structures created a fertile ground for the growth of extremist ideologies. These ideologies often presented themselves as a form of resistance against foreign domination, appealing to those who felt marginalized and disempowered.

The emergence of the Muslim Brotherhood in the 20th century played a significant role in shaping the landscape of religious extremism. Founded in Egypt in 1928, the Muslim Brotherhood sought to establish Islamic states governed by Sharia law. While initially focused on social welfare and education, the organization's political ambitions led to clashes with secular dictators who viewed them as a threat to their power. Repression and persecution of the Muslim Brotherhood only served to fuel its radicalization, pushing some of its members towards violence and extremism.

The Iranian Revolution of 1979 further intensified religious extremism in the region. The establishment of an Islamic Republic in Iran inspired Islamist movements across the Arab world, who saw it as a successful model for overthrowing secular dictatorships. The revolution also deepened sectarian tensions between Sunni and Shia Muslims, leading to a rise in sectarian violence and radicalization.

The United States' involvement in the Middle East, particularly its support for authoritarian regimes, has also contributed to the spread of religious extremism. Perceived as an ally of oppressive governments, the U.S. has often been viewed as an enemy by extremist groups. The U.S. invasion of Iraq in 2003, for instance, created a power vacuum that allowed extremist groups like Al-Qaeda to flourish.

Furthermore, socioeconomic factors such as poverty, unemployment, and lack of education have provided fertile ground for the recruitment of individuals into extremist organizations. Desperate and disillusioned, many turn to radical ideologies as a means of finding purpose and empowerment.

To effectively address the issue of religious extremism in Arab dictatorships, it is crucial to understand its historical roots and the multifaceted factors that contribute to its persistence. By examining the complex interplay between political repression, socioeconomic challenges, and external influences, scholars, politicians, historians, journalists, educators, teachers, and the general public can gain a deeper understanding of the dynamics at play and work towards developing comprehensive strategies for countering religious extremism in the region.

Factors Contributing to the Rise of Radical Ideologies

In recent years, the world has witnessed the rise of radical ideologies within Arab dictatorships. This subchapter aims to shed light on the various factors that have contributed to this phenomenon, highlighting the complexities and challenges faced in the region.

One key factor is the suppression of political dissent and limited avenues for peaceful expression. Arab dictatorships have long been characterized by repressive regimes that quash any form of opposition, leading to frustration and disillusionment among the populace. With limited opportunities for political participation, some individuals turn to radical ideologies as an alternative means of expressing their grievances.

The socio-economic conditions prevailing in Arab dictatorships also play a significant role in fueling radical ideologies. Economic inequality, high unemployment rates, and limited access to basic services create a breeding ground for discontent and hopelessness. Radical ideologies often exploit these grievances, offering a sense of purpose and belonging to individuals who feel marginalized by their governments.

Another contributing factor is the manipulation of media and dissemination of propaganda by Arab dictatorships. By controlling and censoring the flow of information, these regimes can shape public opinion and suppress dissenting voices. However, this control can inadvertently create a vacuum that is filled by radical ideologies, which utilize alternative media channels and online platforms to spread their message.

The failure of international actors to effectively address human rights violations and support democratic movements in the region has also contributed to the rise of radical ideologies. Arab dictatorships often exploit this perceived hypocrisy to portray themselves as defenders of Islam and the Arab world against external threats. This narrative resonates with individuals who feel a sense of pride and identity tied to their religion and culture, leading them to embrace radical ideologies as a means of resistance.

Furthermore, the militarization of Arab dictatorships has had a profound impact on regional security and the rise of radical ideologies. The military plays a pivotal role in maintaining the grip on power by these regimes, often at the expense of civil liberties and human rights. The repression and violence perpetrated by security forces can push individuals towards radical ideologies as a means of self-defense and retaliation against the state.

In conclusion, there are multiple factors contributing to the rise of radical ideologies within Arab dictatorships. The suppression of political dissent, socio-economic inequality, media manipulation, international inaction, militarization, and the failure to transition to democratic systems all intertwine to create an environment conducive to the emergence of radical ideologies. Understanding these factors is crucial for scholars, politicians, historians, journalists, educators, teachers, and the public to address the root causes of radicalization and work towards a more stable and inclusive future in the Arab world.

Countering Religious Extremism and Promoting Tolerance

Religious extremism has emerged as a significant challenge within the context of Arab dictatorships. The combination of repressive political systems and socio-economic grievances has created an environment conducive to the rise of radical ideologies. To address this pressing issue, it is essential for scholars, politicians, historians, journalists, educators, teachers, and the general public to understand the factors contributing to religious extremism and explore strategies for countering it.

One of the key factors leading to the rise of religious extremism in Arab dictatorships is the suppression of political freedoms and lack of channels for peaceful expression. When individuals are denied the opportunity to engage in open political discourse, they may turn to more radical ideologies as a means of expressing their grievances. Therefore, promoting political freedoms and creating spaces for dialogue and peaceful dissent is crucial in combating extremism.

Another contributing factor to religious extremism is the absence of inclusive and tolerant educational curricula. In many Arab dictatorships, religious education is often dominated by a narrow interpretation of Islam, which can foster an exclusivist worldview and fuel extremism. Reforms are needed to promote a more inclusive education system that emphasizes critical thinking, human rights, and interfaith dialogue.

Engaging religious leaders and scholars in countering extremism is also vital. These influential figures can play a significant role in challenging extremist narratives and promoting a more tolerant interpretation of religious teachings. Governments should encourage religious leaders to condemn violence and support initiatives that promote interfaith dialogue and cooperation.

Furthermore, addressing the socio-economic factors that contribute to religious extremism is crucial. Arab dictatorships often struggle with high levels of unemployment, poverty, and inequality. These conditions create fertile ground for radicalization. Governments should prioritize inclusive economic policies that provide opportunities for marginalized communities, particularly the youth, who are most vulnerable to extremist recruitment.

International cooperation and assistance are also crucial in countering religious extremism. Arab dictatorships should work with the international community to share best practices, exchange information, and coordinate efforts in countering extremist ideologies. This includes collaborating on intelligence-sharing, providing technical assistance, and supporting capacity-building initiatives.

Countering religious extremism and promoting tolerance is a complex and multifaceted challenge. It requires a comprehensive approach that addresses the political, socio-economic, educational, and religious dimensions of the issue. By understanding the factors contributing to religious extremism and implementing effective strategies, Arab dictatorships can work towards creating more inclusive and tolerant societies, ultimately contributing to regional stability and security.

Chapter 10: Militarization of Arab Dictatorships: Examining the military's role in maintaining power and its impact on regional security.

The Role of the Military in Arab Dictatorships

In the book "The Arab Dictatorships: The Unfinished Work of the Arab Spring," one of the crucial aspects explored is the role of the military in Arab dictatorships. This subchapter delves into the influence and significance of the military in maintaining power within these authoritarian regimes.

The military has historically played a pivotal role in Arab dictatorships, often acting as the backbone of these oppressive regimes. Scholars, historians, and politicians have long recognized the military's role as a key instrument in suppressing dissent and preserving the status quo. The military's loyalty to the ruling elites is often bought through extensive privileges, financial incentives, and exclusive access to resources and power.

By examining the military's function in Arab dictatorships, it becomes apparent how the armed forces have become deeply intertwined with the political and economic apparatus. The military acts as a guardian of the ruling elites, ensuring their survival and perpetuation of their authority. Its involvement extends beyond defense matters and includes significant control over key sectors of the economy, such as defense industries, construction, and infrastructure projects. This intertwining of military and economic power further solidifies the military's support for the regime.

Moreover, the military in Arab dictatorships often plays a dual role as both an enforcer of the regime's policies and a suppressor of opposition movements. Its extensive intelligence networks and security apparatus enable it to maintain tight control over the population through surveillance, intimidation, and repression. This subchapter explores in depth how the military's involvement in suppressing dissent contributes to the perpetuation of authoritarian rule and the stifling of political freedoms.

The military's role in Arab dictatorships also has significant implications for regional security. Its support for dictatorial regimes can often lead to an escalation of conflicts, both within national borders and across international boundaries. The subchapter analyzes the impact of the militarization of Arab dictatorships on regional stability, highlighting the potential for violent conflicts and the exacerbation of regional tensions.

Understanding the role of the military in Arab dictatorships is essential for scholars, historians, journalists, politicians, and educators. By examining this critical aspect, we can gain valuable insights into the mechanisms of power and the challenges faced by those seeking political change in the region. This subchapter contributes to the broader discussion on Arab dictatorships and their impact on the region's political, social, and economic landscape.

Implications of Militarization on Regional Security

The subchapter titled "Implications of Militarization on Regional Security" delves into the role of the military in Arab dictatorships and its impact on the stability of the region. This topic is of great importance to scholars, politicians, historians, journalists, educators, teachers, and the general public who seek a deeper understanding of the dynamics at play in the Arab world.

Militarization in Arab dictatorships has far-reaching implications for regional security. The military often serves as a tool for maintaining power and control by the ruling elite. The subchapter explores the ways in which the military is used to suppress opposition movements and maintain a tight grip on power. It examines the systematic abuse of human rights and the impact it has on regional stability.

The subchapter also analyzes the dynamics of diplomatic relations and alliances with Arab dictatorships. It delves into how the military's role in maintaining power affects these relationships and the potential consequences for regional security. The subchapter highlights the challenges faced by countries transitioning from dictatorship to democracy and the role of the military in shaping these transitions.

Furthermore, the subchapter addresses the rise of radical ideologies within repressive political systems. It explores the factors contributing to religious extremism in Arab dictatorships and its implications for regional security. The militarization of these regimes often exacerbates tensions and creates a fertile ground for extremist ideologies to thrive.

By examining the implications of militarization on regional security, this subchapter provides valuable insights into the complexities of the Arab world. It sheds light on the challenges faced by opposition movements and the potential for change in these repressive regimes. It also highlights the role of the military in shaping diplomatic relations and its impact on regional stability.

In conclusion, "Implications of Militarization on Regional Security" is a pivotal subchapter in the book "The Arab Dictatorships: The Unfinished Work of the Arab Spring." It addresses the concerns of scholars, politicians, historians, journalists, educators, teachers, and the general public who seek a comprehensive understanding of the factors influencing regional security in Arab dictatorships. By examining the role of the military in maintaining power and its impact on regional stability, this subchapter provides a valuable contribution to the ongoing discourse surrounding the Arab world.

Challenges and Opportunities for Demilitarization

Demilitarization is a crucial aspect of transitioning from dictatorship to democracy in Arab countries that have experienced the Arab Spring. The process of demilitarization involves the reduction of military influence in politics, society, and the economy, and the establishment of civilian control over the armed forces. While demilitarization presents numerous challenges, it also offers significant opportunities for the region's stability and development.

One of the primary challenges in demilitarizing Arab dictatorships is the deep-rooted military influence within the political system. Dictators often rely on the military to maintain their grip on power, leading to a culture of militarism that permeates all aspects of society. Disentangling the military from politics requires a comprehensive approach that addresses legal, institutional, and cultural barriers to civilian control.

Another obstacle to demilitarization is the economic dimension. In many Arab dictatorships, the military has significant control over key sectors of the economy, such as construction, manufacturing, and natural resources. This creates a challenge in reallocating resources and opportunities to civilian sectors, which are essential for economic growth and job creation.

Furthermore, demilitarization faces resistance from vested interests within the military establishment. High-ranking officers may fear losing their privileges and influence if their power is diminished. Overcoming this resistance requires careful negotiation, transparency, and the establishment of alternative career paths and incentives for military personnel to transition into civilian roles.

However, despite these challenges, demilitarization also presents significant opportunities for the region. By reducing military influence, Arab countries can foster the development of democratic institutions, promote the rule of law, and protect human rights. Civilian control over the armed forces is a crucial step towards building accountable and transparent governance systems.

Moreover, demilitarization allows for the reallocation of resources towards social and economic development. By redirecting military spending towards education, healthcare, infrastructure, and job creation, Arab countries can address the root causes of social and economic inequality, which often fuel political instability and social unrest.

Demilitarization also offers an opportunity to rebuild trust between the government and its citizens. The excessive use of force and human rights abuses by the military during the dictatorship era have eroded public confidence. By demilitarizing and establishing civilian oversight mechanisms, governments can restore faith in institutions and promote national reconciliation.

In conclusion, demilitarization is a complex and multifaceted process that presents both challenges and opportunities for Arab dictatorships. While it requires addressing deep-rooted military influence and vested interests, demilitarization offers the potential for democratic consolidation, economic development, and social stability. By embracing demilitarization, Arab countries can lay the foundation for a brighter and more inclusive future.

Chapter 11: Transition Processes in Post-Arab Spring Arab Dictatorships: Investigating the challenges and successes of countries transitioning from dictatorship to democracy.

Lessons Learned from Post-Arab Spring Transitions

The Arab Spring, a series of uprisings that took place across the Arab world in the early 2010s, brought hope for democratic change and the end of oppressive regimes. However, as the dust settled and transitions began, it became clear that the road to democracy was not as smooth as anticipated. This subchapter, "Lessons Learned from Post-Arab Spring Transitions," delves into the valuable insights gained from these experiences, highlighting the challenges, successes, and ongoing work that remains in the aftermath of the Arab Spring.

Scholars, politicians, historians, journalists, educators, teachers, and the public will find this subchapter enlightening as it offers a comprehensive analysis of the transition processes in post-Arab Spring Arab dictatorships. By examining the various experiences and outcomes, readers can gain a deeper understanding of the complex dynamics involved in moving from dictatorship to democracy.

One of the key lessons learned is the importance of inclusive and participatory processes. The Arab Spring movements were largely driven by young people, who demanded a voice in shaping their countries' futures. However, the exclusion of certain groups, such as women and religious minorities, hindered progress and perpetuated inequalities. It is crucial for future transitions to prioritize inclusion and ensure that all segments of society have a say in decision-making processes.

Another lesson is the need for strong institutions and the rule of law. The Arab Spring exposed the weaknesses and vulnerabilities of institutions that had long been under the control of dictators. Building robust institutions that can withstand political turmoil and safeguard democratic principles is essential for sustainable change.

Additionally, the subchapter explores the role of international relations in post-Arab Spring transitions. It highlights the complexities of diplomatic relations and the challenges faced by countries as they navigate their relationships with both regional and global powers.

Furthermore, the subchapter discusses the importance of opposition movements and activism in challenging authoritarian regimes. It examines the various forms of resistance and modes of expression that have emerged, shedding light on the resilience and determination of those advocating for change.

Ultimately, "Lessons Learned from Post-Arab Spring Transitions" offers an in-depth exploration of the challenges and successes of countries transitioning from dictatorship to democracy. It serves as a valuable resource for scholars, politicians, historians, journalists, educators, teachers, and the public, providing them with critical insights into the unfinished work of the Arab Spring and the path forward towards a more democratic and inclusive Arab world.

Challenges in Transitioning to Democracy

The transition from dictatorship to democracy is a complex and arduous process that presents numerous challenges for countries emerging from Arab dictatorships. This subchapter titled "Challenges in Transitioning to Democracy" delves into the difficulties faced by these nations as they strive to establish democratic systems of governance. Scholars, politicians, historians, journalists, educators, teachers, and the public will find this analysis insightful in understanding the intricacies of this transition.

One of the primary challenges in transitioning to democracy is the deep-rooted political culture and institutions established under decades of authoritarian rule. Dictatorships often suppress political opposition, stifle civil society, and manipulate state institutions to consolidate power. Consequently, the establishment of democratic norms, institutions, and practices becomes an uphill battle. This subchapter explores the obstacles faced in dismantling the remnants of the old regime and building a new democratic framework.

Another significant challenge is the lack of experience and political know-how among the post-dictatorship leadership. Many of these leaders may have emerged from opposition movements without prior experience in governance, making it difficult to navigate the complexities of democratic decision-making processes. Furthermore, the absence of a robust civil society and independent media poses obstacles to holding leaders accountable and ensuring transparency.

Socioeconomic challenges also hinder the transition to democracy. Arab dictatorships have often been characterized by economic inequality, with a small elite class accumulating wealth while the majority of the population faces poverty and unemployment. Addressing these disparities and creating inclusive economic systems becomes crucial for building stable and prosperous democracies. This subchapter examines the implications of economic inequality and the potential for social and political instability.

Moreover, the subchapter explores the role of international relations in the transition process. Arab dictatorships often relied on alliances with foreign powers to maintain their grip on power. The impact of these relationships on the transition to democracy and the potential for external interference are analyzed in this section.

Overall, this subchapter sheds light on the multifaceted challenges faced by countries in transitioning from dictatorship to democracy. It provides valuable insights for scholars, politicians, historians, journalists, educators, teachers, and the general public interested in understanding the complexities of this process. By examining these challenges, stakeholders can gain a better understanding of the unfinished work of the Arab Spring and the path towards a more democratic and stable future in the Arab world.

Successful Models of Transition and Democratic Consolidation

In the aftermath of the Arab Spring, the Arab dictatorships have been grappling with the challenges of transitioning from authoritarian rule to democratic governance. While this process has been fraught with difficulties and setbacks, there have been a few successful models of transition and democratic consolidation that offer valuable insights and lessons for other countries in the region.

One such model is Tunisia, often hailed as the only Arab Spring country to have successfully transitioned to democracy. Through a combination of inclusive dialogue, compromise, and strong civil society engagement, Tunisia managed to draft a new constitution, hold free and fair elections, and establish a stable democratic system. The Tunisian experience showcases the importance of a participatory and inclusive transition process, where all stakeholders have a seat at the table and are invested in the success of the democratic project.

Another successful model is Spain's transition to democracy after the fall of the Franco regime. Spain's transition was marked by a strong commitment to national reconciliation, amnesty for political prisoners, and the establishment of institutions that safeguarded democratic principles. The Spanish example highlights the significance of addressing past human rights abuses and fostering a culture of accountability and reconciliation to ensure a stable and enduring democratic system.

South Africa's transition from apartheid to democracy is another notable success story. Through a process of truth and reconciliation, South Africa confronted its painful past and laid the foundation for a multi-racial democratic society. The South African case emphasizes the importance of addressing historical injustices and promoting social cohesion as crucial elements of a successful transition process.

These successful models of transition and democratic consolidation offer valuable insights and lessons for other Arab dictatorships seeking to embark on a similar journey. They underscore the importance of inclusivity, national reconciliation, accountability, and addressing past human rights abuses. Additionally, these models highlight the critical role of civil society, the media, and the international community in supporting and sustaining democratic transitions.

As scholars, politicians, historians, journalists, educators, teachers, and the public, it is essential for us to study and analyze these successful models in order to gain a deeper understanding of the complexities and dynamics of transition processes in post-Arab Spring Arab dictatorships. By doing so, we can contribute to the broader discourse on democratic governance and provide valuable insights to policymakers, activists, and stakeholders involved in promoting political change and stability in the region.

Conclusion: The Unfinished Work of the Arab Spring and the Future of Arab Dictatorships

As we come to the end of this book, it is clear that the Arab Spring was a pivotal moment in the history of the Arab world. It brought about a wave of hope and optimism, as people across the region rose up against their oppressive dictators, demanding freedom, justice, and dignity. However, it is also evident that the work of the Arab Spring is far from finished. The region continues to grapple with the legacy of its dictatorial past and the challenges of transitioning to democracy.

The various chapters in this book have shed light on different aspects of the Arab dictatorships and the obstacles they present to progress. We have examined the role of women in these societies and the progress they have made in their fight for equality, as well as the challenges they continue to face. Economic inequality has also been a significant issue in these countries, with a widening wealth gap threatening social and political stability.

Media suppression and censorship have been tools used by Arab dictators to maintain their power and control over the population. The systematic abuse of human rights has had a devastating impact on regional stability, as individuals and communities have been subjected to violence, torture, and oppression. Opposition movements and activism have emerged as forms of resistance against these authoritarian regimes, but they face immense challenges in their fight for change.

The international relations of Arab dictatorships have also been examined, revealing complex dynamics of diplomatic relations and alliances. Additionally, the role of youth in driving political change and their prospects for a brighter future have been assessed. The rise of religious extremism within these repressive political systems has also been explored, as well as the militarization of these dictatorships and its impact on regional security.

While some countries have made progress in their transition from dictatorship to democracy, many continue to struggle with the challenges of this process. The road to democracy is fraught with obstacles, including corruption, power struggles, and the lingering influence of the old regime.

In conclusion, the Arab Spring brought hope and sparked a desire for change across the Arab world. However, the work is far from over. Scholars, politicians, historians, journalists, educators, teachers, and the public must continue to study, analyze, and engage with the complex issues surrounding Arab dictatorships. Only by understanding these challenges can we hope to contribute to a brighter future for the people of the Arab world, one where freedom, justice, and dignity are not just aspirations, but realities.